Anna Katharina Emmerich, George Richardson

The Nativity of our Lord Jesus Christ

Anna Katharina Emmerich, George Richardson

The Nativity of our Lord Jesus Christ

ISBN/EAN: 9783743336339

Manufactured in Europe, USA, Canada, Australia, Japa

Cover: Foto ©Lupo / pixelio.de

Manufactured and distributed by brebook publishing software (www.brebook.com)

Anna Katharina Emmerich, George Richardson

The Nativity of our Lord Jesus Christ

Preface.

As I am now more than eighty-six years old I don't think it probable that I shall attempt any more translations of Sister Emmerich's revelations. I wish, therefore, to say a few words about dear Sister Emmerich before parting. I have read through her revelations several times during the last sixty years, and I have more frequently read through the New Testament, and have never been able to detect the slightest opposition between them.

The discovery of the House of the Blessed Virgin near Ephesus, exactly corresponding with Sister Emmerich's description of it, has given a new impetus to the desire

Preface.

to read her revelations. This discovery will lead, no doubt, in God's good time, to the finding of our Lady's Tomb, the scene of her glorious Assumption.

The statements made by Sister Emmerich must be regarded only as those of a devout Nun, and must not be confounded with statements of facts supported by the testimony of the Church.

GEORGE RICHARDSON.

Alma Park, Levenshulme.
1899.

THE NATIVITY

Of Our Lord Jesus Christ at Bethlehem.

The Marriage of the Blessed Virgin.

The Holy Virgin lived in the Temple with several other virgins under the charge of pious matrons.

These virgins were occupied with embroidery and other works of the same kind for the hangings of the Temple and the vestments of the priests: they were also employed in washing the vestments and in other matters pertaining to the divine worship. They had little cells whence they had a view of the interior of the Temple, and where they prayed and meditated. When they were arrived at a marriageable age they married. Their parents had given them entirely to God in conducting them to the Temple, and there was among the most pious of the Israelites a secret presentiment that one of these marriages would be the cause some day of the coming of the Messiah.

The Blessed Virgin being fourteen years old, and about soon to leave the Temple and be married, with seven other young girls, I saw St. Anne come to visit her. Joachim was no longer living. When they informed Mary that she must leave the Temple and be married, I saw her deeply moved, declare to a priest that she had no desire to quit the Temple, that she was consecrated to God alone, and had no inclination for marriage : but they told her she must take a husband.

I saw her afterwards in her oratory

pray to God with fervour. I remember also that being very thirsty she descended with her little pitcher to draw water from a fountain or a reservoir, and that there, without any visible apparition, she heard a voice which consoled and fortified her, at the same time making known to her that she must consent to be married.

I saw also a very old priest who was unable to walk — it might be the High Priest. He was carried by other priests into the Holy of Holies, and, whilst he lighted the crifice of incense he read some prayers from a roll of parchment placed on a kind of pulpit. I saw him in an ecstasy. He had a vision, and his finger was placed on the following passage out of the Prophet Isaiah which was written on the roll: "A branch shall arise from the root of Jesse and a flower shall spring from this root" (Isaiah ix. 1).

When the old priest returned to himself he read this passage and knew something by this.

I then saw that messengers were sent to all parts of the country, and that they convoked to the Temple all the men of the race of David who were unmarried. When many of them were assembled in the Temple in their festival dress, they were presented to the Blessed Virgin.

I then saw the High Priest, obedient to an interior impulse which he had received, present branches to each of those present, and tell them to mark each one a branch with his name and hold it in his hand during the prayer and sacrifice. When they had done as required the branches were taken from them and placed upon an altar before the Holy of Holies, and it was announced to them that he among them whose branch should flourish was designed by the

Lord to be the husband of Mary of Nazareth.

Whilst the branches were before the Holy of Holies they continued the sacrifice and the prayer; then after the time fixed, they gave back the branches and announced to them that no one of them was designed by God to become the husband of this virgin.

Afterwards the priests of the Temple sought afresh in the registers of families if no other descendant of David was in existence whom they had overlooked. As they there found an indication of six brothers of Bethlehem, of whom one was unknown and had been absent for a long time, they inquired after the abode of Joseph, and discovered him a short distance from Samaria, in a place situated near a small river, where he dwelt on the margin of the water, working for a master carpenter.

On the order of the High Priest Joseph came to Jerusalem and presented himself at the Temple. They made him also hold in his hand a branch while they prayed and offered sacrifice. As he was offering to place it on the altar before the Holy of Holies, there came out from it a white flower like a lily, and a luminous apparition descended upon him. It was as if he had received the Holy Ghost. They knew then that St. Joseph was the man designed by God to be the spouse of the Blessed Virgin, and the priests presented him to Mary in the presence of her mother. Mary, resigned to the will of God, humbly accepted him as her spouse, for she knew that everything is possible with God, who had received her vow of belonging only to Him.

Concerning the Marriage and the Wedding Dress of Mary and Joseph.

Sister Emmerich, in her daily visions on the ministry of Our Lord, saw on Monday the 24th of September, 1821, Jesus teaching in the synagogue of Gophna, and there staying with the family of a chief of the synagogue, a relative of Joachim. She heard on this occasion two widows, daughters of this man, conversing together on the marriage of the parents of Jesus, at which they had assisted in their youth, with other relatives, and she communicated what follows. As the two widows referred in their conversation to the marriage of Mary and Joseph, I saw a picture of the marriage, and I was struck with the beauty of the nuptial dress of the Holy Virgin. The marriage of Mary and Joseph, which was kept up for seven or eight days, was celebrated at Jerusalem, in a house near Mount Sion, which was frequently let for similar occasions. Besides the witnesses and companions of Mary in the School of the Temple, there were many relatives of Anne and Joachim, and amongst others a family of Gophna, with two daughters. The marriage was solemn and sumptuous. Many lambs were killed and offered in sacrifice. I saw Mary very distinctly in her bridal dress. She had a very large gown, open in front, with large sleeves. This gown had a blue ground strewed with red, white, and yellow roses, intermingled with green leaves, like the rich chasubles of ancient times—the lower border was trimmed with fringe and tassels. Over her dress she wore a mantle of celestial blue, which had the appearance of a large sheet. Besides this mantle, the Jewish women frequently carry also on certain occasions a species of mourning mantle with sleeves —the mantle of Mary fell back over her shoulders and terminated in a train.

She carried in her left hand a small crown of red and white roses made of silk. In her right hand she held, in form of a sceptre, a beautiful gilt candlestick, without a foot, surmounted by a little dish where something was burning, which produced a white flame.

The virgins of the Temple arranged the hair of Mary—many of them were engaged at it, and it was done in an incredibly short time. Anne had brought the wedding dress, and Mary, in her humility, would not consent to wear it after her marriage—her hair was fastened round her head, and they put on her a white veil, which hung below her shoulders, and a crown was placed over this veil. The Holy Virgin had an abundance of hair of a light gold colour; her eyebrows black and elevated; large eyes, habitually cast down, with long black eyelashes; a nose of a beautiful form, rather long; a noble and graceful mouth, and a slender chin. She was of middle stature. She walked, clad in her rich costume, with much grace, elegance, and gravity. She afterwards put on for her marriage another dress, less splendid, of which I possess a small piece among my relics. She wore this striped dress at Cana and on other solemn occasions. She sometimes put on her marriage dress to go to the Temple. There were rich people who changed their dress three or four times for their marriage. In her dress of ceremony Mary rather resembled certain illustrious ladies of later times; for instance, the Empress St. Helen and even St. Cunegonda, though she differed from them in the cloak which Jewish women usually wear, and which more resembled that of the Roman ladies. There were at Sion, in the neighbourhood of the cenacle, a certain number of women who prepared beautiful stuffs—

all kinds—which I remarked in consequence of these dresses.

Joseph had a long and very wide robe of a blue colour; the sleeves, which were very large, were fastened at the side with strings. Round the neck he wore a kind of brown collar, or rather a large stole, and over his breast two white bands hung down. I have seen all the ceremonies of the marriage of St. Joseph and the Blessed Virgin—the marriage feast and other solemnities.

Mary's Marriage Ring.

On the 29th of July, 1821, Sister Emmerich had a vision on the grave clothes of our Lord Jesus Christ, and the wonderful prints of His body, which showed themselves miraculously upon the winding sheet in which He had been wrapped. As on this occasion she found herself conducted to several places, where these holy relics were found, some religiously preserved, others forgotten by men and honoured only by the angels or certain holy souls, she believed that she saw preserved in one of these places the marriage ring of the Blessed Virgin, and she then related as follows:

I have seen the marriage ring of the Blessed Virgin. It is neither silver, nor gold, nor any other metal: it is of a dark colour with changing reflections; it is not a small circle, it is as thick and as wide as a finger. I saw it quite smooth and still, as if encrusted with small regular triangles where there were letters. I saw it kept under several locks in a beautiful church—there were some pious people, who before celebrating their marriage touched their marriage rings with it.

On the 21st of August, 1821, she said:

I have learned during the last few days many details relative to the history of the marriage ring of Mary, but I cannot relate them all in order. I have seen to-day a festival in a church in Italy where it is found. It is exposed in a kind of monstrance, which was placed above the tabernacle. There was there a large altar, richly decorated, with many ornaments in silver. I saw that they touched the monstrance with several rings.

I saw during the festival, on the two sides of the ring, Mary and Joseph appear in their bridal dresses. It seemed to me that St. Joseph placed the ring on the finger of the Blessed Virgin. I saw the ring all luminous and as if in motion.*

* When the writer wrote this on the 4th of August, 1821, he could not understand why the Sister had this vision precisely on the 3rd of August. He was much surprised many years afterwards when he read in a Latin writing on the ring of the Blessed

When the marriage was finished Anne returned to Nazareth and Mary departed also, in company of several virgins who had quitted the Temple at the same time as she did. I do not know how far these virgins conducted her on her way. The first place at which they stayed to pass the night was at the School of the Levites at Betheron. Many made the journey on foot. Joseph, after the marriage, went to Bethlehem to regulate some family affairs. It was not until later that he returned to Nazareth.

Virgin, preserved at Perouse, that they exhibited this ring to the people on the 3rd of August, of which probably neither he nor the Sister knew anything. He found this information on page 39 of the writing entitled, "Of the Marriage Ring of the Blessed Virgin, Mother of God, religiously preserved at Perouse" (The Commentator of S. B. Laurus of Perouse, 1626).

From the Return of Mary to the Annunciation.

Before relating the vision of the Annunciation the Sister communicated two fragments of previous visions, of which we can only offer a conjectural explanation. Being still very feeble through the effects of a serious illness, she related what follows some time after the marriage of the Blessed Virgin and St. Joseph.

There was a festival in the house of St. Anne, and some children assembled with Joseph and Mary round a table on which were placed some glasses.

The Blessed Virgin had a striped mantle with red, blue, and white flowers, as we see on ancient chasubles. She wore a transparent veil, and above this a black veil. This *fête* appeared to be connected with the marriage festivities.

She related no more on this subject,

and we can only suppose that this repast took place when the Blessed Virgin left her mother, after the arrival of St. Joseph, and retired with him into the house at Nazareth. The following day she related what follows.

To-night in my contemplation I sought for the Blessed Virgin, and my conductor led me into the house of St. Anne, every part of which I recognised. I found there neither Joseph nor Mary. I saw St. Anne preparing to go to Nazareth, where the Holy Family was now residing. She carried under her arm a packet which she was taking to Mary. She went to Nazareth, crossing a plain and a little wood placed on an eminence. I went there also. The house of St. Joseph was not far from the gate of the city. It was not so large as the house of St. Anne. A square well, which was down some steps, was in the neighbourhood, and there was before the house a small square court. I saw St. Anne visit the Blessed Virgin, to whom she gave what she had brought with her. I saw Mary weep very much, and for some time accompany her mother who was returning to her home. I saw St. Joseph in front of the house in a secluded spot.

We may gather from these fragments that Anne visited for the first time her daughter at Nazareth, and brought her a present. Mary, who now lived by herself, separated from her well-beloved mother, shed tears of tenderness in parting from her.

The Annunciation.

On the 25th of March, 1821, the Sister said :

I saw the Blessed Virgin soon after her marriage, in the house of Joseph at

Nazareth, to which my guide conducted me. Joseph had departed with two asses. I think it was to fetch something that he had inherited, or to bring the tools of his trade. He seemed to me still on his journey.

Besides the Blessed Virgin and two young women of her own age, who had been, I believe, her companions in the Temple, I saw in the house St. Anne with the widow, her relative, who was in her service, and who later on followed her to Bethlehem after the birth of Jesus. St. Anne had renewed everything in the house.

I saw the four women walking about in the house, and then walk together in the court. Towards evening I saw them re-enter and pray standing round a little round table, after which they ate some herbs which had been brought there. They separated afterwards. St. Anne still went about here and there in the house, like the mother of a family engaged in her duties. The two young persons went into their separate chambers, and Mary also retired into her own.

The chamber of the Blessed Virgin was at the back of the house, near the fireplace; it was reached by three steps, for the ground at this part of the house was higher than the rest, and on a rocky foundation. Opposite the door the chamber was round, and in this circular part, which was separated by a partition of the height of a man, was the bed of the Blessed Virgin, rolled up. The walls of the chamber were covered to a certain height with a kind of inlaid work, made of pieces of wood, of different colours. The ceiling was formed by parallel joists, the spaces between which were filled with wicker work, ornamented with figures of stars.

I was conducted into this chamber by the young man of shining appearance who always accompanies me,* and I will relate what I saw as well as such a wretched person as I am can do.

The Blessed Virgin on entering dressed herself, behind the screen of her bed, in a long robe of white wool, with a large belt, and covered her head with a veil of light yellow. In the meantime the servant entered with a light, lighted a lamp with several branches which hung from the ceiling, and retired. The Blessed Virgin then took a little low table which stood against the wall, and placed it in the middle of her chamber. It was covered with a red and blue cloth, in the middle of which a figure was embroidered. I cannot say whether it was a letter or an ornament. A roll of parchment, written upon, was on the table.

* Her guardian angel.

The Blessed Virgin having arranged it, between the place of her bed and the door, on a spot where the floor was covered with a carpet, placed before it a small round cushion on which to kneel. She then knelt down, her two hands leaning upon the table. The door of the chamber was in front of her, to the right. She turned her back to her couch.

Mary let down the veil over her face, and joined her hands before her breast, but without crossing the fingers. I saw her pray for a long time with great ardour, her face turned towards heaven. She invoked the redemption, the coming of the King promised to the people of Israel, and she asked also to have some part in this coming. She remained a long time on her knees transported in ecstasy. She then bent her head over her breast.

Then from the ceiling of the chamber descended, on her right side, in a slightly oblique direction, such a mass of light that I was obliged to turn myself towards the court, where the door was placed. I saw then in this light a resplendent young man, with white flowing hair, descend before her, through the air. It was the Angel Gabriel. He spoke to her, and I saw the words come from his mouth like letters of fire. I read them and understood them. Mary slightly turned her veiled head to the right side. Notwithstanding, in her modesty she did not look at him. The angel continued to speak. Mary turned her face on one side, as if in obedience to an order, slightly raised her veil, and replied. The angel spoke again. Mary completely raised her veil, looked at the angel, and pronounced the sacred words: "Behold the handmaid of the Lord; be it done to me according to thy word."

The Blessed Virgin was in a profound ecstasy; the chamber was full of light. I saw no more the light of the lamp which was burning, neither did I see the ceiling of the room. Heaven appeared to be open; my observation followed the luminous way above the angel. I saw at the extremity of this river of light the Holy Trinity. It was like a luminous triangle whose rays reciprocally penetrated each other. I then recognised what we must adore, but can never express — the omnipotent God, Father, Son, and Holy Ghost, and yet one only God Almighty.

When the Holy Virgin had said, "Be it done to me according to thy word," I saw a winged apparition of the Holy Spirit, which, however, had not completely the ordinary representation under the form of a dove. The head had something like the human face; the light spread out on both sides like wings, and I saw come from it as it were three luminous streams towards the right side of the Blessed Virgin, where they were reunited; then this light penetrated her right side, the Blessed Virgin herself became luminous, and as if transparent: it seemed as if everything that was opaque in her retired before this light, as night before the day. She was at this moment so inundated with light that nothing in her appeared obscure or opaque; she was resplendent and as if completely illuminated.

I afterwards saw the angel disappear; the luminous ray from which he had emerged retired; it was as if heaven drew it in and caused to re-enter into itself this flood of light.

After the disappearance of the angel I saw the Blessed Virgin in a profound ecstasy and altogether recollected in herself. I saw that she knew and adored the Incarnation of the Saviour in herself, where He was as a small luminous human body, completely formed, and provided with all His members. Here at Nazareth everything is completely otherwise than at Jerusalem. At Jerusalem the women have to remain in the vestibule, they cannot enter into the Temple—priests only have access to the sanctuary—but at Nazareth it is a virgin, who is herself the Temple. The Holy of Holies is within her, the High Priest is within her, and she is alone with Him. How touching and wonderful is this, and yet how simple and natural. The words of David in the 45th Psalm are accomplished: "God is in the midst thereof (His tabernacle), and it shall not be moved." It was a little past midnight when I saw this mystery. After some time St. Anne entered into Mary's room with the other women: a marvellous movement in nature had awakened them, a luminous cloud had passed over the house. When they saw the Blessed Virgin on her knees under the lamp transported in ecstasy in prayer, they respectfully retired.

In contemplating this night the mystery of the Incarnation I was also instructed in many other things. Anne received an interior knowledge of what had been accomplished.

I learned why the Redeemer would remain nine months in the womb of His mother and become an infant; why He had not desired to come into the world a man, like our first father, and show Himself in all His beauty, like Adam coming from the hands of his Creator—but I cannot clearly explain this. That which I now understand is that He wished to sanctify again the conception and the birth of men, which had been so much degraded by original sin. If Mary became His mother, and that He did not come sooner, was that she alone was what no creature was before or after her, the pure vessel of grace which God had promised to men, and in whom He would become man, to pay the debt of human nature by means of the superabundant merits of His passion. The Blessed Virgin was the perfectly pure flower of the human race unfolded in the fulness of time. All the children of God amongst men, all those who since the beginning had laboured in the work of their sanctification had contributed to His coming. She was the only pure gold of the earth. She alone was the pure and spotless portion of the flesh and blood of the whole human race, who, prepared, purified, gathered, and consecrated through all the generations of her ancestors, conducted, protected, and fortified under the regulations of the law of Moses, was finally produced as the fulness of grace. She was predestined in eternity and she has appeared in time as the Mother of the Eternal.

The Blessed Virgin was a little more than fourteen at the time of the Incarnation of Jesus Christ. Jesus Christ arrived at the age of thirty-three years and three times six weeks. I say three times six because the figure six was shown to me at this instant, but repeated three times.

When Joseph returned to Nazareth with the Blessed Virgin after her visit to her cousin Elizabeth, he saw by her figure that she was enceinte. He was then assailed with all sorts of troubles and doubts, for he knew nothing of the visit of the angel to Mary. Soon after his marriage he had gone to Bethlehem on some family affairs. Mary in the meantime had returned to Nazareth with her parents and some companions. The angelical salutation had taken place before the return of Joseph to Nazareth. Mary in her timid humility had kept to herself the secret of God.

Joseph, full of trouble and anxiety, did not attempt to learn anything from without, but struggled in silence against his doubts. The Blessed Virgin, who had perceived this, at once was grave and pensive, which increased still more the anxiety of Joseph.

When they had arrived at Nazareth I saw that the Blessed Virgin did not go at once into the house with St. Joseph. She remained two days with a family connected with her own. They were the parents of the disciple Parmenas, who was not then born, and who afterwards became one of the seven deacons in the first community of Christians at Jerusalem.

These people were allied to the Holy Family; the mother was the sister of the third husband of Mary Cleophas, who was the father of Simeon, Bishop of Jerusalem. They had a house and garden at Nazareth. They were also allied to the Holy Family on the side of Elizabeth. I saw the Blessed Virgin remain some time with them before returning to Joseph's house; but his trouble increased to such an extent, that when Mary desired to return to his house, he had formed the intention of leaving it and going away secretly. Whilst he was meditating on this project an angel appeared to him in a dream and consoled him.

PREPARATIONS FOR THE BIRTH OF JESUS CHRIST.—DEPARTURE OF THE HOLY FAMILY FOR BETHLEHEM.

SUNDAY, the 11th of November, 1821.— For many days past I have seen the Blessed Virgin near her mother, St. Anne, whose house is about a league from Nazareth, in the Valley of Zabulon. Her servant remained at the house of Nazareth. She attends to St. Joseph when Mary is with her mother. In reality, so long as Anne lived, they had not an entirely separate establishment, but received always from the latter everything they required.

I saw, during fifteen days, the Blessed Virgin engaged in preparations for the birth of Jesus Christ; she got ready coverlets, bandages, and swaddling clothes. Her father, Joachim, was no longer living. There was in the house a little girl of about seven years old who was often near the Blessed Virgin, and to whom she gave lessons. I believe that she was the daughter of Mary of Cleophas. She was also called Mary. Joseph is not at Nazareth, but he will soon arrive. He is on his return from Jerusalem, where he had led victims for sacrifice.

I saw the Blessed Virgin in the house. She was in an advanced state of pregnancy, and was working sitting in a room with several other women. They were preparing articles and coverlets for the confinement of Mary. Anne had considerable property in cattle and pasture lands. She furnished the Blessed Virgin abundantly with everything which was needful for her condition : as she believed that Mary would be confined at her house, and that all her relatives would visit her on this occasion, she made all sorts of preparations for the birth of the child of promise. They prepared for this purpose beautiful coverlets and rugs.

I had seen a coverlet of this kind at the time of the birth of St. John, in the house of Elizabeth. It had on it symbolical figures and sentences worked by the needle. In the middle was a sort of wrapper in which the woman when lying in, was placed. When the different parts of the coverlet were fitted together around her with strings and buttons she seemed like a little child in its swaddling clothes, and could easily sit up between the cushions, and receive the visits of her friends, who would sit round her on the border of the tapestry.

They got ready also in the house of St. Anne things of this kind, besides bandages and swaddling clothes for the child. I saw also threads of gold and silver, which they interwove here and there. All these articles and coverlets were not only for the use of the person confined; there were also many things intended for the poor, whom they always thought of, on such occasions. I saw the Blessed Virgin and other women sitting on the floor round a large chest, and working at a larger coverlet, which was placed on this box in the midst of them. They made use of short sticks, to which thread of different colours was attached. St. Anne was very busy; she went here and there to get the wool, to divide it, and give their work to her servants.

Monday, the 12th of November.—Joseph should return to-day to Nazareth. He was at Jerusalem, whither he had led some animals for sacrifice. He had left them at a small inn, situated a quarter of a league from Jerusalem and kept by an old couple without children. They were pious people with whom persons could stay with all confidence. Joseph went from there to Bethlehem; but he did not visit the relatives he had there. He wished only to get information relative to a numbering or a levy of duty, which required that every one should come to the place where he was born. He did not, however, report himself; as he intended, when the time of the purification of Mary was accomplished, to go with her from

Nazareth to the Temple at Jerusalem, and thence to Bethlehem, where he intended to settle. I do not know what advantage he expected from this; but he did not like living at Nazareth. It was on this account that he took advantage of this opportunity to go to Bethlehem.

He there got information about stones and wood used by carpenters, as he had the intention to build a house. He returned afterwards to the inn near Jerusalem, conducted the victims to the Temple and returned home.

As to-day towards midnight he was crossing the Plain of Kimki, six leagues from Nazareth, an angel appeared to him and told him to depart with Mary for Bethlehem, for it was there that she should bring her child into the world. The angel also directed what he should take with him: that he must take but few things, and especially not the embroidered coverlets. He must also, besides the ass on which Mary would ride, take with him an ass of a year old who had not had young; he must let it run at liberty, and always follow the road which it took.

This evening Anne went to Nazareth with the Blessed Virgin. They knew that Joseph was coming; they appeared, however, not to know that Mary would go to Bethlehem. They believed that Mary would bring her child into the world in the house at Nazareth, for I saw that they brought there many things which they had prepared packed in matting. Joseph will arrive at Nazareth in the evening.

Tuesday, the 13th of November.—To-day I saw the Blessed Virgin Mary with her mother in the house at Nazareth, when Joseph informed them of what had been said to him on the preceding night. They returned together to Anne's house, and I saw them make preparations for a speedy departure. Anne was much distressed. The Blessed Virgin knew already that she must bring forth her son at Bethlehem, but through humility she said nothing.

She knew this from the prophecies on the birth of the Messiah, which she kept at Nazareth. She had received these writings from her mistresses in the Temple, and these holy women had explained them to her. Her ardent desire continually invoked the coming of the Messiah; she called blessed, her who should bring into the world this holy infant, and desired only to be the least of her servants. She did not think in her humility that this honour could be destined for her. As she knew by the text of the prophecies that the Saviour would be born in Bethlehem, she conformed with still greater joy to the Divine will, and prepared for this journey, a very painful one at this season, for it was often very cold in the valleys between the chains of mountains.

This evening St. Joseph and the Blessed Virgin, accompanied by Anne, Mary of Cleophas, and some servants, departed from St. Anne's house. Mary was sitting on the saddle of an ass which also carried the luggage. Joseph led the ass. There was another ass on which Anne intended to return.

Journey of the Holy Family.

This morning I saw the holy travellers arrive at six leagues from Nazareth, at a plain called Ghinim, where the angel had appeared to St. Joseph the evening before. Anne possessed some pastures at this place, and the servants were to bring from this place the ass of a year old, which Joseph had to take with him : it ran sometimes in advance of the travellers, sometimes close to them. Anne and Mary of Cleophas here bid good-bye to the holy travellers and returned with the servants.

I saw the Holy Family proceed further by a road which rises towards the mountains of Gilboa. They did not go into cities, and followed the young ass, which always took cross ways. It was in this manner that I saw them at some property of Lazarus, a short distance from the village of Ghinim, by the side of Samaria. The superintendent received them in a friendly manner. He had known them on another journey. Their family had connections with that of Lazarus. There were there beautiful orchards and walks. The position was so elevated as to command a very extensive view. Lazarus inherited this property from his father. Our Lord Jesus Christ stayed often here during

His ministry, and taught in the vicinity. The manager and his wife conversed in a friendly manner with the Blessed Virgin, and showed their surprise that she should have undertaken so long a journey in her present condition, when she could have remained so comfortably at her mother's house.

Night of Thursday or Friday, the 16th of November.—I saw the Holy Family at some leagues beyond the spot mentioned above, proceeding in the night towards a mountain through a very cold valley. It seemed to have been a white frost. The Blessed Virgin suffered much from the cold, and she said to St. Joseph, "We shall be obliged to stop here; I can't go any further." Scarcely had she said these words when the young ass stopped all at once under a large and very old fir tree which was near the place and near which was a spring. They halted under this tree.

Joseph arranged with wrappers a seat for the Blessed Virgin, whom he assisted to alight from the ass and she sat against the tree. Joseph hung up a lantern which he carried with him on a bough of the tree. I have frequently seen persons who travel at night in this country do the same. The Blessed Virgin called upon God, and asked that He would not permit the cold to be hurtful to him. Then she all at once perceived such a great heat that she stretched her hands to St. Joseph that he might warm his. They refreshed themselves a little with the small cakes and the fruits which they had with them, and drank of the water from the neighbouring fountain, in which they mixed some of the balm which Joseph had brought in a little pitcher. Joseph consoled and encouraged the Holy Virgin. He was so good: he suffered so much because the journey was so painful to her. He spoke to her about the good lodgings which he expected to procure at Bethlehem: he knew of a house belonging to some very honest people, where they could be well accommodated at reasonable expense. He praised Bethlehem in general, and said anything he could to console her. This gave me anxiety, as I knew things would turn out otherwise.

To this place on their journey they had passed two small streams of water, one of them by a high bridge, and the two asses had passed through the ford. The young ass, which ran at liberty, had singular ways of proceeding. When the road was well defined, for instance, between two mountains, and they could make no mistake, sometimes it ran behind the travellers, sometimes a long way before them. When the way divided it always reappeared and took the right direction; when they desired to stop, it stopped of itself, as at their rest under the fir tree. I do not know whether they passed the night under this tree or reached another resting-place.

This fir tree was an old and sacred tree which had formed part of the Wood of Moreh, near to Sichem. Abraham coming from the land of Chanaan, had there seen the Lord appear, who had promised him this land for his posterity. He had erected an altar under this fir tree. Jacob, before going to Bethel to offer sacrifice to the Lord, had buried under this fir tree the idols of Laban, and the jewels which his family had with them. Joshua had erected there the tabernacle in which was the Ark of the Covenant, and had there assembled the people and made them renounce their idols. It was there also that Abimelech, the son of Gideon, had been proclaimed King by the Sichemites.

Friday, the 16th of November.—To-day the Holy Family arrived at a large farm, two leagues more to the south than the fir tree. The mistress of the house was absent, and the master refused to receive St. Joseph, telling him that he could easily go further on. When they had gone a short way further they found the young ass in the cottage of a shepherd, into which they also entered. Some shepherds, who were engaged arranging the cottage, received them with much kindness. They gave them some straw and small bundles of rushes and branches to make a fire. The shepherds went to the house from which they had been sent away; and when they told the mistress of this house how Joseph appeared to be good and pious, and his wife was beautiful and had a saintly appearance, she reproached her husband for having driven away such excellent persons.

I saw this woman also soon go to the cabin where the Blessed Virgin was staying; but she dare not enter through timidity, and returned to her house to get some food.

The place where they were now staying was on the northern side of a mountain, a short distance between Samaria and Thebez. To the east of the place beyond the Jordan is Succoth. Ainon is a little more to the south also beyond the river. Salem is on this side—it would be about twelve leagues from there to Nazareth.

After a time the woman came with two children to see the Holy Family, bringing with her some provisions. She excused herself politely, and seemed touched with their position. When the travellers had eaten and taken some rest the husband came also and begged pardon of St. Joseph for having sent him away. He advised him to go another league towards the top of the mountain; telling him that he would arrive at a good resting-place before the beginning of the Sabbath, and could remain there during the day of rest: they then set forward on their journey.

When they had travelled nearly a league always mounting upwards, they arrived at an inn of decent appearance, composed of several buildings surrounded with gardens and trees. These were also, ranged like espaliers, trees which yielded balm: this place of accommodation was also on the northern side of the mountain.

The Blessed Virgin had dismounted. Joseph led the ass. They came near the house and St. Joseph asked the host to accommodate them; but he declined because his inn was full. His wife then came, and as the Blessed Virgin addressed herself to her, and asked her with the most touching humility to give them a lodging, this woman experienced a profound emotion, and the host also would no longer refuse. He arranged a convenient shelter for them in an adjoining cabin and put their ass into the stable. The young ass was not there; it was running about at liberty in the neighbourhood. It was always at a distance from them when not wanted to show the way.

Joseph prepared a lamp under which he placed himself at prayer with the Blessed Virgin, observing the Sabbath with a touching piety. They ate something and reposed on mats spread on the ground.

Saturday, the 17th of November.—Today I saw the Holy Family rest in this place all the day. Mary and Joseph prayed together. I saw the wife of the host with her three children near the Blessed Virgin. The woman who had received them on the previous day came also to visit her with her two children ; they sat near her in a very friendly manner, and were touched with the modesty and wisdom of Mary. The Blessed Virgin talked to the children and gave them instructions.

The children had little rolls of parchment : Mary made them read, and spoke to them in such a kind way that they could not help looking at her. It was affecting to see, and still more affecting to hear. I saw St. Joseph in the afternoon take a walk with his host in the environs : this is what I have always seen done by pious country people on the Sabbath-day. The holy travellers remained still in this place during the following night.

Sunday, the 18th of November.—The good hosts of this place had conceived an incredible affection for the Blessed Virgin, and showed a tender compassion for her state. They entreated her in the most friendly manner to remain with them, and to await the time of her delivery; they showed her a convenient room which they desired to give her. The woman offered from the bottom of her heart all her assistance and friendship.

But they resumed their journey early in the morning, and descended by the south-east side of the mountain into a valley. They went then further from Samaria, to which the route they had till then taken seemed to lead them. As they descended the mountain they could see the Temple on Mount Garizim. It could be seen from a great distance. There were many figures of lions and other animals on the top, which shone in the sunbeams.

I saw them travel about six leagues to-day. Towards evening, being in a plain south-east of Sichem, they entered into a rather large house of shepherds, where they were well received. The master of the house was charged with the supervision of the orchards and fields which belonged to a neighbouring town. The house was not completely in the plain, but on a slope. Here everything was fertile and in a better condition than the country which they had previously passed. It was turned towards the sun, which in the land of promise makes a considerable difference at this time of the year. From here to Bethlehem there were many similar dwellings of shepherds dispersed in the valleys.

The people of this place were some of those shepherds whose daughters many of the servants of the three kings, who remained in Palestine, subsequently married. From one of these marriages came a young boy, whom Our Lord cured in this same house, at the prayer of the Blessed Virgin, on the 31st of July (7th of the month of Ab), in the second year of His ministry, after talking with the woman of Samaria. Jesus took him and two other young men to accompany Him on the journey which He made into Arabia after the death of Lazarus, and he became later on a disciple of the Lord. Jesus frequently stayed and taught here. There were children in the house: Joseph blessed them before his departure.

Continuation of the Journey to Bethlehem.

Monday, the 19th of November.—To-day I saw them follow a more regular road. The Blessed Virgin travelled on foot from time to time. They found more frequently convenient resting-places where they refreshed themselves. They had with them little loaves and a beverage both refreshing and strengthening, in little pitchers of a very elegant shape which had two handles and shone like bronze. It was balm, which they mixed with water. They gathered also berries and fruits which still hung upon the trees and bushes in certain places exposed to the sun. Mary's seat on the ass had a sort of ledge on the right and left on which to rest the feet, so that they did not hang down as those of country people who go on horseback in our country. Her movements were singularly proper and becoming. She sat alternately on the right and left. The first thing that St. Joseph did when they halted or entered any place was to find some place where the Blessed Virgin could conveniently sit down and rest. He often washed his feet, as did Mary. In general, they frequently washed themselves.

It was already night when they arrived at an isolated house, but the master of the house would not open it; and when

St. Joseph represented the state of Mary, who was not in a condition to go any further, adding that he did not expect to be lodged for nothing, this hard-hearted and rude man replied that his house was not an inn, and desired them to leave him quiet and give over knocking, and things of that sort. This boorish man did not even open his door, but gave his rude reply behind the closed door. They then continued their way and after some time they entered into a shed near which they found that the little ass had stopped. Joseph procured a light and prepared a couch for the Blessed Virgin who helped him. He brought the ass in also, for which he prepared a litter and forage. They prayed, took a little food, and slept some hours. From the last inn to here they had travelled about six miles of the way. They were now about twenty-six leagues from Nazareth and ten from Jerusalem. So far they had not followed the highway, but had crossed many ways of communication which went from the Jordan to Samaria and joined the principal routes which led from Syria into Egypt. The cross roads which they had followed were very narrow on the mountains; they were sometimes so strait that it required every care to proceed without stumbling: but the asses walked with a very sure step. Their present resting-place was in a level country.

Tuesday, the 20th of November.— They left this place before daylight. The way again became slightly hilly. I believe they came near the road which led from Gabara to Jerusalem and which formed at this spot the boundary between Samaria and Judea. They were again rudely driven away from a house when they were some leagues to the north-east of Bethania. It happened that Mary, being very tired, wished to take something and to rest; then Joseph turned off from the road to go about half a league from there to a spot in which there was a beautiful fig tree which was generally covered with fruit. This tree was surrounded with seats to rest upon, and Joseph knew of it from one of his previous journeys. But when they arrived there they did not find a single fruit, which troubled them very much. I have a confused recollection that later on Jesus met with this tree, which was covered with leaves, but bore no fruit. I believe that the Lord cursed this tree on a journey which He made after escaping from Jerusalem, and that it entirely withered away.*

* The Sister was so unwell when she related this that she could not clearly point out in what place this fig tree grew, which, however, is not the fig tree mentioned by the Evangelist.

They then came to a house where the master began by treating in a brutal manner St. Joseph, who humbly asked hospitality. He looked at the Blessed Virgin by the light of his lantern, and rallied St. Joseph for bringing his young wife with him. But the mistress of the house came forward: she pitied the Blessed Virgin, and in a friendly manner offered them a room in a building adjoining the house, and even brought them some small cakes. The husband repented of his brutality, and showed himself very obliging to the Holy Family.

They subsequently went to a third house, inhabited by a young family. They received them, but without much courtesy; they scarcely took notice of them. These people were not among the shepherds of simple manners, but like rich country people of the place, altogether taken up with their affairs, business, etc.

Jesus visited one of these houses after His baptism, the 20th of October. They had made an oratory of the room where His parents had passed the night. I cannot well say whether it was the house where the master had rallied St. Joseph. I only confusedly remember that they had made this arrangement after the miracles which marked the birth of the Saviour.

Joseph made frequent halts towards the end of their journey, for the Blessed Virgin became more and more fatigued. They followed the road which was shown them by the young ass, and made a circuitous route of a day and a half to the east of Jerusalem. The father of Joseph had owned pastures in this country, and he knew it well. If they had directly crossed the desert, which is to the south, behind Bethany, they could have reached

Bethlehem in six hours; but the road was mountainous and very inconvenient at this season. They followed, then, the young ass through the length of the valleys, and went a little towards the Jordan.

Wednesday, the 21st of November.—To-day I saw the holy travellers enter in the daytime into a large house of shepherds. This must be about three leagues from the place where John baptised in the Jordan and about seven leagues from Bethlehem. This is the house where thirty years after Jesus passed the night, the 11th of October, the eve of the day on which for the first time after His baptism He passed before John the Baptist. Near this house was a separate barn, where they kept their tools and such things as the shepherds made use of. In the court was a fountain surrounded with baths which received the water of this fountain through pipes. The master of this house must have had a large property: there was there an extensive cultivation of land. I saw a number of servants come and go, who there took their meals.

The master of the house received the travellers in a very friendly manner, and showed himself very obliging. He took them into a comfortable room and took care of the ass. A servant washed the feet of St. Joseph at the fountain and gave him other clothes whilst he cleaned his own, which were covered with dust. A female servant rendered the same assistance to the Blessed Virgin. They took their repasts in this house and slept here. The mistress of the house was a very frivolous character, and she remained shut up in her room. She looked at the travellers without being seen; and as she was young and vain, the beauty of the Blessed Virgin displeased her. She feared also that Mary would speak to her, desire to stay in her house and be confined there; so she had the want of politeness not to show herself, and took measures that the travellers should depart on the following day. This was the woman whom, thirty years after, Jesus found in this house blind and bent double, and whom He cured, after having given her some advice on her want of hospitality and her vanity. There were also some children in the house. The Holy Family passed the night there.

Thursday, the 22nd of November.—To-day towards noon I saw the Holy Family quit the place where they had stayed the previous night. Some of the people of the house went with them a part of the way. After a short journey of about two leagues they arrived towards the evening at a place which crossed a highway bounded on each side by a long row of houses with courts or gardens. Joseph had relatives living here. It seemed to me that they were the children of the second marriage of his step-father or his step-mother. These houses had a handsome appearance. They passed, however, this place from one end to the other; then, about half a league from there, they turned to the right in the direction of Jerusalem, and arrived at a large inn, in the court of which was a fountain with many conduits. There were many people assembled together celebrating a funeral.

The interior of the house, in the centre of which was a fireplace with a tunnel for the smoke, had been transformed into a large apartment by the taking away of the movable partitions which ordinarily constituted several rooms; behind the fireplace were suspended some black hangings and in the front stood something which resembled a bier covered with black. There were several men praying there; they wore long black robes and over these shorter white ones. Some of them had a kind of black maniple with fringe fastened to the arm. Some women were in another room completely covered by their vestments. They sat on some low chests and were weeping. The master of the house, altogether engaged in the funeral ceremonies, only made signs for the travellers to enter: but the servants received them very well and took care of them; they prepared for them a separate lodging with suspended mats which much resembled a tent. Later on I saw the hosts visit the Holy Family and talk with them in a friendly way. They had no longer on their white vestments. Joseph and Mary, after having taken a little food, prayed together and took their rest.

Friday, the 23rd of November.—To-day

towards noon Joseph and Mary set forward on their journey to Bethlehem, from which they were about three leagues distant. The mistress of the house pressed them to stay, as it appeared to her that Mary might be delivered at any moment. Mary replied, after having lowered her veil, that she had still thirty-six hours to wait. I am not sure that she did not say thirty-eight. This woman would have taken care of them without any charge; not, however, in her own house, but in another building. I saw when they were leaving that Joseph spoke to the host about his asses: he praised them very much, and said he had taken the young ass with him in order that he might pledge it in case of necessity. As his host spoke of the difficulty of getting lodgings in Bethlehem, Joseph told him he had friends there and was sure of being well received. It always gave me pain to hear him speak with confidence of the good reception that awaited him: he spoke of it again to Mary on the journey. It is clear that even holy persons may be deceived.

BETHLEHEM.—ARRIVAL OF THE HOLY FAMILY.

FRIDAY, the 23rd of November.—The distance of the way from their last resting-place to Bethlehem would be about three leagues; they made a circuitous route at the north of Bethlehem and approached the city on the south side. They made a halt under a tree outside of their route. Mary dismounted from the ass and put her clothes in order; then Joseph proceeded forward with her towards a large building surrounded with other smaller buildings and courts. They were still a few minutes from Bethlehem. There were trees there, and many people were preparing tents all about. It was an old house belonging to the family of David, and which had belonged to Joseph's family. Some relatives or acquaintances of Joseph lived there still; but they treated him like a stranger, and would not recognise him. This was now the house where they received the taxes for the Roman Government. Joseph, accompanied by the Blessed Virgin, and holding the ass by the bridle, proceeded to this house, for all persons who arrived were bound to make it known there, and they there received a billet without which they were not allowed to enter Bethlehem.

The Sister said afterwards, with some intervals in her statement: The young ass is no longer with them; it runs round the city towards the south: there was there a little valley. Joseph has entered into the large building. Mary is in a little house with some women; they are very kind to her, and give her something to eat. These women cook for the soldiers: they are Roman soldiers, who had straps round their loins. The season is very pleasant here, and not very cold. The sun is seen above the mountain, which is between Jerusalem and Bethania. They have here a most beautiful view. Joseph is in a large room which is not on the ground floor: they ask him who he is, and they consult the large scrolls which are hanging on the walls; they unfold them, and read there his genealogy and also that of Mary. They did not appear to know that she also, by Joachim, descended in a direct line from David. The man asked him where his wife was.

It is six years since the people of this country had been regularly taxed. There had been a good deal of disorder and confusion. This impost had been two months in operation : it had been paid from time to time during the past seven years, but not regularly; it has now to be paid double. Joseph has arrived rather late for the payment of the duty, but they have treated him very politely. He has not yet paid. They asked him what were his means of subsistence, and he replied that he had no landed property—that he lived by his trade, and that he also received assistance from his mother-in-law.

There were a great many writers and important officials in the house : in the upper part were Romans and many soldiers; there were also Pharisees, Sadducees, priests, elders, and a number of Scribes and functionaries, both Jews and Romans. There was no meeting of this kind at Jerusalem, but in several other parts of the country; for example, at Magdalum, near the Lake of Gennesareth, where the people of Galilee came to pay as well as the people of Sidon, in consequence, as I believe, of certain commercial arrangements. It is only those who have no landed property who are obliged to go to the place of their birth.

The produce of the tax for the next three months will be divided into three parts, of which each has a different destination. The first is for the benefit of the Emperor Augustus, Herod, and another prince who dwelt in the neighbourhood of Egypt. He had taken part in a war and possessed certain rights over a portion of the country, and on this account something had to be paid to him. The second part was for the building of the Temple; it seemed to me that it had to be applied to pay off a debt. The third part should be for the widows and the poor, who have received nothing for a long while; but, as happens nowadays, the money scarcely ever goes to the right persons. Good pretexts are given for raising the duty, and almost all remains in the hands of powerful people.

When what concerned St. Joseph was arranged they made the Blessed Virgin also come before the writers; but they did not read their papers to her. They told St. Joseph that he need not have brought his wife with him, and they had the appearance of joking with him about the youth of Mary, which caused him slight confusion.

Joseph in vain seeks for a Lodging.— They go to the Grotto of the Crib.

They then entered into Bethlehem, in which the houses were separated from each other by considerable spaces. They entered across some rubbish and by a gate which was fallen into decay. Mary remained quietly with the ass at the end of the street, and Joseph searched in vain for a lodging in the first houses, for there were many strangers in Bethlehem and many people were running here and there. He returned to Mary and told her that he could find nowhere to lodge there, and that they must go on further into the city. He led the ass by the bridle whilst the Blessed Virgin walked by his side. When they were come to the end of another street Mary remained again near the ass while Joseph went from house to house without being able to find one where they would receive him. He soon returned very much troubled. This was repeated several times, and sometimes the Blessed Virgin had a long time to wait : everywhere the place was taken up, everywhere he was repulsed, and he ended by telling Mary that they must go to another part of Bethlehem, where they would be sure to find what they wanted. They then retraced their steps in the direction contrary to that which they had taken in coming when they turned to the south. They then passed through a street which seemed rather a country road as the houses were isolated and on slight elevations.

Arrived at the other side of Bethlehem, where the houses were still more scattered, they found a large empty space situated in a hollow; it was like a deserted field in the city. There was there a kind of shed, and a short distance from it a large tree, like a lime tree, with a smooth trunk, whose branches extended widely and formed a kind of roof over it. Joseph led the Blessed Virgin to this tree; he arranged a convenient seat for her with bundles at the foot of the trunk, in order that she might rest whilst he sought again for a lodging in the neighbouring houses. The ass stood still with its head turned towards the tree. Mary remained at first standing, leaning against the trunk of the tree. Her robe of white wool had no belt, and fell about her in folds; her head was covered with a white veil. Many persons passed by and looked at her, not knowing that their Saviour was so near them. How patient, humble, and resigned she was. She had to wait a long time, and at last she sat down upon the rugs, her hands joined on her breast, and with her head bowed down. Joseph returned to her in great trouble; he had not found a lodging. The friends of whom he had spoken to the Blessed Virgin would scarcely notice him. He shed tears, and Mary consoled him. He went again from house to house; but as, in order the more to induce them to consent, he had spoken of the near approach of his wife's confinement, this drew upon him a more distinct refusal. The place was solitary; but in the end some people passing by looked from a distance with curiosity, as is usual if any one is seen remaining a long time in the same place towards the close of the day. I believe that some of them spoke to Mary and asked her who she was. At last Joseph returned; he was so much troubled that he hardly dare come near her. He told her it was of no use, but that he knew further on in the city a spot where the shepherds often stayed when they came to Bethlehem with their flocks, and that they would find there at least a shelter. He knew the place from his youth: when his brothers tormented him he had often retired there to escape from their persecutions. He said if the shepherds came there he could easily arrange with them, but that they were rarely here at this season of the year. He added, when they were quietly settled he would make further inquiries. They then went away by the eastern side of Bethlehem, following a deserted path which turned to the left. It was a road like one which is found in walking by the side of the dilapidated walls, ditches, and fortifications of a small city in ruins. The road at first rose a little, it then descended the slope of a small hill, and led them a few minutes to the east of Bethlehem, before the place they were seeking, near a hill or an old rampart, in front of which stood some trees. They were green trees (firs or cedars), and other trees which had little leaves like box leaves.

I have learned many things which took place in ancient times in the Grotto of the Crib. I remember only that Seth, the child of promise, was there conceived and brought into the world by Eve, after a penitence of seven years.

It was there that the angel told her that God had given her this offspring in the place of Abel. Seth was concealed and nourished in this grotto and in that of Maraha, for his brothers sought his life as the children of Jacob did that of Joseph. At a more recent epoch, when men lived in these grottos, I have often seen them make excavations in the stone so that they and their children could sleep there comfortably on the skins of beasts or on beds of grass. The excavation made in the rock under the crib probably served for the bed of Seth, or the subsequent occupiers of the grotto. Of this, however, I am not sure.

The Holy Family enter into the Grotto of the Crib.

FRIDAY, the 23rd of November.—It was already late when they arrived at the entrance to the grotto. The young ass which, since they had entered into the paternal house of Joseph, had run about all round the city, came there to meet them, and began joyfully to leap about near them. The Blessed Virgin then said to Joseph: "See, it is certainly the will of God that we go in here." Joseph placed the ass under a kind of roof which there was before the entrance of the grotto: he prepared a seat for the Blessed Virgin and she sat down upon it whilst he went to procure a light at the entrance of the grotto. The entrance was partially obstructed by bundles of straw and mats placed against the walls. There were also in the grotto many things which were in the way, and Joseph cleared them away so as to prepare a convenient place for the Blessed Virgin on the eastern side of the grotto. He fastened a lighted lamp to the wall and brought Mary in, who placed herself on a couch of rest which he had prepared for her with coverlets and some bundles. He excused himself very humbly for only being able to procure her such a poor lodging, but Mary inwardly was contented and joyful.

When she was properly settled Joseph went out with a leathern bottle, which he carried with him, behind the hill, into the meadow where a small brook was flowing. He filled the bottle with water and brought it into the grotto. He then went into the city and procured some small dishes and some charcoal. The Sabbath was near, and in consequence of the numerous strangers who required a number of indispensable articles, they had set up tables at the corners of the streets on which there were provisions that might be required. I believe there were there people who were not Jews.

Joseph returned carrying the lighted charcoal in a kind of grated box. He placed them at the entrance of the grotto, lighted the fire with a small piece of dry wood, and then brought the repast, which consisted of small cakes and some dry fruits. When they had eaten and prayed Joseph prepared a couch for the Blessed Virgin. He spread over a litter of rushes a coverlet similar to those which I had seen in the house of St. Anne, and placed another rolled-up coverlet to support her head. After having brought in the ass and fastened it to a spot where it would be out of the way, he stopped up the openings of the grotto by which the air came in, and arranged a place to sleep for himself in the entrance of the grotto.

When the Sabbath commenced he remained with the Blessed Virgin under a lamp and recited with her the prayers of the Sabbath: he then quitted the grotto and went into the city. Mary wrapped herself up to take some rest. During the absence of Joseph I saw the Blessed Virgin pray on her knees: then she stretched herself on the coverlet reposing on her side; her head reposed upon her arm which was placed upon the pillow. Joseph returned later on: he prayed again and humbly placed himself on his bed at the entrance of the grotto.

Saturday, the 24th of November.—To-day the Sister was very unwell and could only say very little. She communicated, however, as follows:

The Blessed Virgin passed the Sabbath in the Grotto of the Crib praying and meditating with great fervour. Joseph went out sometimes: he probably went to the synagogue of Bethlehem. I saw them eat the food prepared on the preceding day and pray together. In the afternoon, at which time the Jews generally take a walk on the Sabbath-day, Joseph led the Blessed Virgin to the Grotto of the tomb of Maraha, the nurse of Abraham. She remained some time in this grotto which was more spacious than that of the crib; and where Joseph arranged a seat for her. She stayed also under the tree which stood near, always praying and meditating until the close of the Sabbath. Joseph then brought her back. Mary had told her husband that the birth of the child would take place on this day at midnight, for at that hour would terminate the nine months which had passed since the salutation of the angel of the Lord: she had prayed him to do all they could to honour in the best manner the entrance into the world of the child promised by God and supernaturally conceived. She had asked him also to pray with her for those hard-hearted people who had refused to give him hospitality. Joseph offered the Blessed Virgin to get some pious women of Bethlehem whom he knew to come and assist her. She did not wish it, and she told him she should have no need of help from any one.

Joseph went to Bethlehem before the close of the Sabbath, and as soon as the sun was set he bought some things which he required: a dish, a small low table, some fruits and dried grapes, which he brought to the Grotto of the Crib: he went from thence to the Grotto of Maraha and led back the Blessed Virgin to that of the crib, where she sat upon the coverlet. Joseph prepared some food: they ate and prayed together. He put up a division between the place which he had chosen to sleep in and the rest of the grotto by means of some poles, on which he hung some mats which he found there. He gave the ass which was fastened to the wall of the grotto something to eat: he then filled the manger of the crib with reeds and grass and moss and spread a coverlet over it.

As the Blessed Virgin had then told him that her time was at hand, and wished him to pray in his chamber, he suspended several lighted lamps from the roof and went out from the grotto as he had heard a noise near the entrance. He there found the young ass, which till then had been running about in the valley of the shepherds. It appeared very joyful and played and jumped about him: he fastened it under the shed, which was before the grotto, and gave it some food.

When he returned to the grotto, and before entering his retreat, he cast his eyes upon the Blessed Virgin. He saw her praying on her knees before the couch:

her back was turned towards him and she was looking towards the east. She seemed to him as if surrounded by flames, and all the grotto seemed to shine with a supernatural light. He looked at it as Moses when he saw the burning bush: then seized with a holy fear, he entered into his cell and prostrated himself with his face to the ground.

The Birth of Christ.

The light which surrounded the Blessed Virgin became more and more brilliant: the light of the lamp prepared by Joseph could not be seen. When the hour of midnight arrived Mary was transported in an ecstasy. I saw her raised a certain height from the ground; she had her hands crossed upon her breast. The light kept increasing around her; everything seemed to feel a joyful emotion, even things inanimate. The rock which formed the floor and the wall of the grotto were, as it were, alive with light. But soon I saw no more of the roof; a luminous path, whose brightness continually increased, went from Mary to the highest heaven. Then was there a marvellous movement of the celestial glories, which, approaching nearer and nearer, appeared distinctly under the form of the angelic choirs. The Blessed Virgin, raised from the earth in her ecstasy, prayed and turned her eyes to her God, of whom she had become the mother, and who, a feeble new-born infant, was lying on the ground before her.

I saw Our Saviour like a little shining infant, whose brilliance eclipsed all the surrounding splendour, lying upon the rug before the knees of the Blessed

Virgin. He seemed to me very small, and to grow larger before my eyes; but this was only the radiance of a light so dazzling that I can scarcely say how I could see it.

The Blessed Virgin remained some time in ecstasy. Then I saw her place a linen cloth over the child; but she did not touch Him nor take Him yet into her arms. After a short time I saw the Infant Jesus move, and I heard Him cry. It was then that the Blessed Virgin recovered the use of her senses. She took the child, wrapped it in the linen cloth with which she had covered it, and took it in her arms against her breast. I believe that she suckled it. I then saw angels around her in human form prostrate themselves before the new-born and adore Him.

About an hour had elapsed since the birth of the child, when Mary called St.

Joseph, who was still praying with his face to the ground. Approaching, he prostrated himself, full of joy, humility, and fervour. It was only when Mary had induced him to press to his heart the sacred gift of the Most High, that he rose, received the Infant Jesus in his arms, and returned thanks to God with tears of joy.

Then the Blessed Virgin swathed the Infant Jesus. Mary had only four linen cloths with her. I then saw Mary and Joseph sitting on the ground near each other. They did not speak, but seemed absorbed in contemplation. Before Mary, swathed as an ordinary child, was laid the new-born Jesus, beautiful and bright as lightning. "Ah!" I exclaimed, "this place contains the Salvation of the whole world, and no one can doubt it."

They then placed the infant in the crib. They had re-filled it with rushes and beautiful plants, on which they had spread a coverlet. It was above the trough, hollowed in the rock to the right of the entrance to the grotto, which became larger there in a southerly direction. When they had placed the infant in the crib they both stood at the side, shedding tears of joy and chanting songs of praise. Joseph then arranged the sleeping couch and seat of the Blessed Virgin by the side of the crib. I saw her, both before and after the birth of Jesus, dressed in a white garment, which completely covered her. I saw her during the first days sitting, kneeling, standing, or even lying on her side, and sleeping; but neither ill nor fatigued.

THE "GLORIA IN EXCELSIS." — THE BIRTH OF CHRIST ANNOUNCED TO THE SHEPHERDS.

I SAW in many places, even in the most distant countries, an unusual joy and an extraordinary movement during this night. I saw the hearts of many good men animated with a joyous desire, and those of the wicked full of anguish and trouble. I saw many animals show their joy by their movements, the flowers raise their heads, plants and trees receive as it were new life and spread far and wide their perfumes. I saw also springs burst out of the ground. Thus at the moment that the Saviour was born an abundant spring burst forth in the grotto which is on the hill to the north of the Grotto of the Crib. Joseph saw it on the following day and prepared a place for it to run off. Over Bethlehem the sky was of a sombre red, whilst over the Grotto of the Crib, in the valley near the Grotto of Maraha, and over the Valley of the Shepherds there was a shining vapour.

In the Valley of the Shepherds, about a league and a half from the Grotto of the Crib, there was a hill at which vineyards commenced which extended from thence as far as Gaza. The cottages of three shepherds, who were the heads of the families of shepherds who lived in the neighbourhood, stood on the side of this hill. At a distance twice that from the Grotto of the Crib, was a tower called the Shepherd's Tower: it was a large pyramid shaped scaffolding of woodwork, having for its base blocks of stone placed in the midst of green trees, and built upon an isolated hill standing in the midst of the plain. It was surrounded with staircases and galleries, with a kind of small round towers, the whole being as it were hung round with matting. It had some resemblance to those towers of wood from the top of which they observed the stars in the country of the three Magi kings, and which had in the distance the appearance of a large ship with many masts and sails. There was a very extensive view from this tower over the surrounding country. Jerusalem, and even the Mountain of the Temptation in the Desert of Jericho could be seen from here. The shepherds had watchers there to look after the movements of their flocks, and to warn them by sounding a horn, in case of an incursion of robbers or soldiers, and whom they could see for a long distance from this spot.

The families of the shepherds lived all about here within a radius of more than two leagues; they occupied small isolated farms surrounded with gardens and fields. The place where they assembled together was near this tower. The guardians appointed to watch over the common property dwelt here on the side of the hill where the tower stood; there were cottages, and separate from these a large shed with many apartments, where the wives of the guardians lived and prepared the food. On this night I saw the flocks near the tower; a part were in the open air, another part were under a shed near the hill of the three shepherds.

When Jesus was born I saw the three shepherds struck with the unusual aspect of this marvellous night. Standing near their cottages, they looked round and observed with wonder an extraordinary light above the Grotto of the Crib. I saw also that the shepherds who were near the tower were excited. I saw them mount the scaffolding and look towards the side of the Grotto of the Crib. While the three shepherds had their eyes turned towards heaven, I saw a luminous cloud descend before them. As it came near I observed a movement. I saw forms and figures become visible, and I heard harmonious songs of a joyful kind, and which became more and more distinct. The shepherds were at first afraid; but an angel appeared before them and said: "Fear not; I come to announce to you great joy for all the people of Israel: for to-day is born for you in the city of David a Saviour who is Christ the Lord. And this is the sign by which you shall know Him: you shall find an infant wrapped in swaddling clothes, and laid in a manger." Whilst the angel announced this the splendour increased all around him, and I saw six or seven large figures of angels, beautiful and shining. They had in their hands something like a long streamer, whereon was written something in large letters of the size of a hand, and I heard them praise God and sing: "Glory to God in the highest heavens, and on earth peace to men of good will."

The shepherds of the town had the same apparition, but a little later. The angels also appeared to a third group of shepherds near a fountain, situated three leagues from Bethlehem to the east of the Shepherd's Tower. I did not see the shepherds go immediately to the Grotto of the Crib, from which one part of them were a league and a half distant, and the others double that distance.

The Sister saw during the night of the Nativity many things touching the precise determination of the time of the birth of Christ; but her state of sickness and the visits which were paid to her on the day following, which was the festival of St. Catherine, her patron Saint, caused her to forget a good deal. However, a short time afterwards, being in an ecstasy, she communicated some fragments of her visions, when it is remarkable that she always saw the numbers written in Roman letters, and that she had often difficulty in reading them; but she explained them, repeating the name of the letters in the order in which she saw them, or she traced them with her fingers: this time, however, she told the numbers.

You can read it, she said, it is marked there. Jesus Christ was born before the year of the world 3997 was ended; afterwards the four years, less a portion of a year, which elapsed between the Nativity and the end of the year 4000 were forgotten, for subsequently they have made our new era commence four years later.

One of the Consuls of Rome was then named Lentutus: he was the ancestor of St. Moses, priest and martyr, of whom I have here a relic, and who lived in the time of St. Cyprien. Also the Lentutus who became the friend of St. Peter in

Rome was descended from him. Herod had reigned forty years. During seven of those years he was not independent, but he already oppressed the country and practised great cruelty. He died, if I mistake not, in the sixth year of the life of Jesus. I believe that his death was kept secret for some time. He was sanguinary up to the time of his death, and in his last days did much evil. I saw him drag himself along into a large room all cushioned. He had a lance at hand and tried to strike those who came near him. Jesus was born a little before the thirty-fourth year of his reign. Two years before Mary entered the Temple, Herod made some erections in it. It was not a new Temple which he made, only changes and decorations. The flight into Egypt took place when Jesus was nine months old, and the Massacre of the Innocents when He was still in His second year. She mentioned also several circumstances and several facts from the life of Herod which show how she saw everything in detail; but it was impossible to put into order what she had related at broken intervals.

The birth of Jesus Christ took place in a year in which the Jews reckon thirteen months. It is an arrangement analagous to that of our bissextile years. I believe also that the Jews have twice in the year months of twenty and twenty-two days. I understood something of this in reference to their festival days, but of this I have only a confused recollection. I remarked also that several times they made changes in the calendar. This was at the time of their coming out of the captivity, when they were working at the Temple. I saw the man who changed the calendar and I have known his name.

Adoration of the Shepherds.

Sunday, the 25th of November.—At the first break of day the three principal shepherds came from their little hill to the Grotto of the Crib, with the presents which they had prepared. They were little animals very much resembling roe deer: if they were small goats they differed from those of our country. They had long necks and beautiful shining eyes; they were very graceful and nimble in their pace. The shepherds led them along attached to thin cords: they also carried on their shoulders birds which they had killed, and other birds under their arms of a larger size.

They knocked timidly at the door of the Grotto of the Crib and Joseph came to meet them. They repeated to him what the angels had announced to them, and told him that they were come to pay their homage to the infant of promise and to present Him with their offerings. Joseph accepted their presents with humble gratitude, and conducted them to the Blessed Virgin, who was sitting near the crib and holding the Infant Jesus on her knees. The three shepherds knelt down humbly and remained a long time in silence absorbed in feelings of indescribable joy. They afterwards sang the canticle which they had heard the angels sing and a psalm which I have forgotten. When they wished to retire the Blessed Virgin gave them the little Jesus, whom they held in their arms one after another. Then, weeping, they gave Him back to her and quitted the grotto.

Sunday, the 25th of November, in the evening.—The Sister was during the whole of this day in great suffering, both physical and mental. This evening, being just asleep, she found herself transported to the Promised Land; as, independently of her contemplations of the Nativity, she had besides a series of visions on the first year of the ministry of Jesus, and precisely at the same time on the fast of forty days she exclaimed with naïve astonishment: "Ah, how touching is this! I see on one side Jesus at the age of thirty years fasting and tempted by the devil in a cavern of the desert; and on the other side I saw Him a new-born babe, adored by the shepherds in the Grotto of the Crib." After these words she rose from her bed with surprising rapidity, ran to the opened door of her chamber, and as if intoxicated with joy, called the friends who were in the anteroom, saying to them: "Come, come quickly, and adore the infant who is near me." She then returned to her bed with the same rapidity, and began, whilst her face shone with enthusiasm and fervour, to sing in a clear and marvellously expressive voice the *Magnificat*, the *Gloria in Excelsis*, and other unknown canticles in a simple style of profound meaning and partly in rhyme. She sang the seconds also of one of these airs. There appeared in her an emotion of joy singularly touching. This is what she related on the following morning:

Yesterday evening many shepherds, with their wives and even their children, came from the Shepherd's Tower, which is four leagues from the grotto. They brought birds, eggs, honey, skeins of thread of different colours, small packets resembling raw silk, and bouquets of a plant resembling the rush, and which had large leaves. This plant had ears full of large grains. When they had given their presents to Joseph they humbly approached the crib and, kneeling, they sang some very beautiful psalms—the *Gloria in Excelsis* and some short canticles I sang with them. They sang in several parts, and in one of these I took the second. I remember very nearly the following words: "Oh, little infant, red as the rose, you appear as the messenger of peace." When they took leave they bent over the crib, as if they embraced the little Jesus.

Monday, the 26th of November.—I saw to-day the three shepherds assist in turn St. Joseph to arrange everything conveniently in the Grotto of the Crib and in the side grottos. I saw also near the Blessed Virgin several pious women, who rendered her different services. They were Esseniens, who lived a short distance from the Grotto of the Crib, in a hollow situated to the south of the hill. They occupied near together a sort of chambers hollowed in the rock, some distance from the ground. They had small gardens near their houses, and instructed the children of their sect. It was St. Joseph who had induced them to come. He knew this society ever since his youth; for when he fled from his brothers to the Grotto of the Crib he had more than once visited these pious women. They came one after another to the Blessed Virgin, bringing small quantities of provisions, and busied themselves with the cares of the household for the Holy Family.

Tuesday, the 27th of November.—This day I saw a very touching scene in the Grotto of the Crib. Joseph and Mary were standing near the crib, and looking on the Infant Jesus with deep tenderness. All at once the ass threw himself on his knees and bent his head to the ground. Mary and Joseph shed tears. This evening a message came from St. Anne. An old man came from Nazareth with a widow relative of St. Anne, and who was her servant. They brought several little things for Mary. They were very much moved at the sight of the infant; the old servant man shed tears of joy. They soon set out on their way to carry the news to St. Anne. The female servant remained with the Blessed Virgin.

Wednesday, the 28th of November.—To-day I saw the Blessed Virgin with the Infant Jesus and the servant leave the Grotto of the Crib for several hours. I saw her conceal herself in the side grotto, where a spring of water had burst forth after the birth of Jesus Christ. She remained nearly four hours in this grotto, where subsequently she spent two days. Joseph, at the break of day, had so arranged it that she could stay there without great inconvenience. They went there in consequence of an inward admonition that several persons would come to-day from Bethlehem to the Grotto of the Crib. I believe they were emissaries of Herod.

In consequence of the shepherds' conversation, the report had spread about that something miraculous had taken place at this spot at the time of the birth of a child. I saw these men exchange words with St. Joseph, whom they found before the grotto with the shepherds; and they left him sneeringly when they had seen his poverty and simplicity. The Blessed Virgin, after having remained about four hours in this side grotto, returned to the crib with the Infant Jesus.

The Grotto of the Crib enjoyed a sweet tranquillity. Nobody came from Bethlehem; the shepherds alone were in communication with it. The apparition to the shepherds at the hour of the birth of Jesus had caused that all the good people of the valleys had heard speak of the marvellous child of promise. They came now to honour the infant.

Friday, the 30th of November.—To-day many shepherds and other good people came to the Grotto of the Crib and honoured the Infant Jesus with great emotion.

When everybody was gone away for the synagogue of Bethlehem, Joseph got ready in the grotto the lamp for the Sabbath, which had seven wicks, lighted it, and placed it on a little table on which were scrolls containing prayers, and under this lamp he celebrated the Sabbath with the Blessed Virgin and the servant of St. Anne.

Monday, the 3rd of December.—This evening I saw Elizabeth come from Juttah to the Grotto of the Crib, riding on an ass, which was led by an old servant. Mary and she embraced with feelings of inexpressible joy. She pressed the Infant Jesus to her heart, shedding tears. The Blessed Virgin related to her cousin everything which had happened to her up to the present time, and when she spoke of what she had suffered in seeking for a lodging at Bethlehem Elizabeth wept with all her heart.

During the preceding days I have often seen Mary show her child to some visitors covered with a veil and quite naked, with the exception of the cloth round His body. At other times I have seen Him completely swathed.

THE END.

www.ingramcontent.com/pod-product-compliance
Lightning Source LLC
Chambersburg PA
CBHW020148170426
43199CB00010B/944